Chinese Spiritual Thoughts

Chinese Spiritual Thoughts

Healing the Soul with
the Tao Te Ching

Kevin M. Thomas

CHINESE SPIRITUAL THOUGHTS
Healing the Soul with the Tao Te Ching
Kevin M. Thomas

KETNA Publishing
P.O. Box 90861 Burton, Michigan 48509

Copyright © 2018 by Kevin M. Thomas

All rights reserved. No part of this book may be reproduced or transmitted in any form or by any means, electronic or mechanical, including photocopying, recording or by any storage or retrieval system without permission in writing from copyright author.

For more information, address to KETNA Publishing
P.O Box 90861, Burton, Michigan 48509

First KETNA Printing Edition 2018

Cover Design By: 99Designs
Book Design By: Medlar Publishing Solutions Pvt Ltd., India
Proofreading By: Kelly Bixler and Sean Burns
of www.thewriteproofreader.com

is a registered trademark of KETNA Publishing

Printed in the USA

Library of Congress Control Number: 2017917735
ISBN: 978-0-9963874-9-1 (Softcover)
ISBN: 978-1-948265-00-3 (hard cover)
ISBN: 978-1-948265-01-0 (ebook)

Dedication

This book is dedicated to God, for he is the very reason I live. Next, it is dedicated to those seeking the truth of the *Tao Te Ching*, for these are the very people seeking a better path. Next, to my parents, June and Grover, who showed me compassion when I needed it most. To my children, Isiah, Caroline, Kimberly and Cheyenne, the truth and my unconditional love for you keeps me going. To loyal friends and family who have supported me, especially all those reading this book, I hope that it brings you a blessing and deeper understanding of togetherness, love, peace, wisdom, and understanding. Finally, I dedicate this book to those who seek common ground among various beliefs. As a Christian, I believe that it is important to find things of value across many faiths, and perhaps find a message that can unite us all as human beings trying to make the world a better place.

"When I am with those who are weak, I share their weakness, for I want to bring the weak to Christ. Yes, I try to find common ground with everyone, doing everything I can to save some."
   1 Corinthians 9:22

Acknowledgments

To God, for he is the reason for my existence and all my effort.

To my parents June and Grover, who gave me a sanctuary so I could survive and write.

To my children, Isiah, Caroline, Kimberly, and Cheyenne: The unconditional love in my heart for you keeps me alive and moving forward.

To those who wanted a solid translation of the *Tao Te Ching*, you inspired me.

To those supportive friends and family and those in the trenches that made this book possible, I thank you.

Table of Contents

Introduction . . . . *xii*

Chapter One 1
Chapter Two 2
Chapter Three 3
Chapter Four 4
Chapter Five 5
Chapter Six 6
Chapter Seven 7
Chapter Eight 8
Chapter Nine 9
Chapter Ten 10
Chapter Eleven 11
Chapter Twelve 12
Chapter Thirteen 13
Chapter Fourteen 14
Chapter Fifteen 15
Chapter Sixteen 16
Chapter Seventeen 17
Chapter Eighteen 18

Chapter Nineteen 19
Chapter Twenty. 20
Chapter Twenty-One. 21
Chapter Twenty-Two. 22
Chapter Twenty-Three. 23
Chapter Twenty-Four 24
Chapter Twenty-Five. 25
Chapter Twenty-Six. 26
Chapter Twenty-Seven. 27
Chapter Twenty-Eight. 29
Chapter Twenty-Nine 30
Chapter Thirty 31
Chapter Thirty-One 32
Chapter Thirty-Two 33
Chapter Thirty-Three 35
Chapter Thirty-Four 36
Chapter Thirty-Five. 37
Chapter Thirty-Six 38
Chapter Thirty-Seven 39
Chapter Thirty-Eight. 40
Chapter Thirty-Nine 42
Chapter Forty 44
Chapter Forty-One 45

Chapter Forty-Two	47
Chapter Forty-Three	49
Chapter Forty-Four	50
Chapter Forty-Five	51
Chapter Forty-Six	52
Chapter Forty-Seven	53
Chapter Forty-Eight	54
Chapter Forty-Nine	55
Chapter Fifty	56
Chapter Fifty-One	57
Chapter Fifty-Two	58
Chapter Fifty-Three	59
Chapter Fifty-Four	60
Chapter Fifty-Five	61
Chapter Fifty-Six	63
Chapter Fifty-Seven	64
Chapter Fifty-Eight	66
Chapter Fifty-Nine	67
Chapter Sixty	68
Chapter Sixty-One	69
Chapter Sixty-Two	70
Chapter Sixty-Three	72
Chapter Sixty-Four	74

Chapter Sixty-Five. 76
Chapter Sixty-Six 77
Chapter Sixty-Seven 78
Chapter Sixty-Eight. 80
Chapter Sixty-Nine 81
Chapter Seventy 82
Chapter Seventy-One 83
Chapter Seventy-Two 84
Chapter Seventy-Three 85
Chapter Seventy-Four 87
Chapter Seventy-Five 88
Chapter Seventy-Six 89
Chapter Seventy-Seven 90
Chapter Seventy-Eight 91
Chapter Seventy-Nine. 92
Chapter Eighty 93
Chapter Eighty-One 94

About the Author *96*
Chinese Spiritual Thoughts *97*

Introduction

Despite writing both a paraphrased version and a interpretation of this great work, I was seeking to write a more direct translation—an English translation as close to the original text as possible, yet understandable to seekers of the truth.

So let's begin with the background. The *Tao Te Ching* is the second-most translated book in the world, next to the Bible, and is currently made up of eighty-one brief chapters. Its growing popularity cannot be denied, and it has become the foundation for Chinese religion, Chinese philosophy, and Taoism itself. It has also influenced other schools like legalism, Confucianism, and of course, Buddhism. It is often cited as a source of creativity, and has inspired many artists and millions of people around the world.

The *Tao Te Ching* is also known as the Daodejing, Dao De Jing, and the DaodeJing. It was written by Laozi (Old Master), believed to be a contemporary of Confucius. Some believe that he was a grand historian in China who lived for 996 years. Others believe that the text was written by more than one author.

Then there are the different texts. The first manuscripts were written on ancient bamboo, silk, and paper, and likely written in seal script, clerical script, or regular script styles. Because of the lack of grammatical particles, many of the translations seemed to contradict themselves, or at least be open to various interpretations. Additionally, it was translated over 250 times in various western languages, which can create more confusion. Said Homer Welch, "It is a famous puzzle, which everyone would like to feel he had solved."

In fact, the Chinese themselves have at least three main translated versions of the *Tao Te Ching*: the *Yan Zun Version* (80 BC–10AD), the *Heshang Gong Version* (180–157 BC), and the *Wang Bi Version* (226–249AD).

There have been some exciting discoveries along the way, including some manuscripts found by explorer Marc Aurel Stein in the Mogao Caves in the 1920's and 1930's that date back to 270 CE.

In 1993, the oldest version of the text was found in a tomb near Guodian; it was written on bamboo tablets, and was dated prior to 300 BCE. This find revealed fourteen unknown verses or chapters.

There may also be a connection to western religion. Christian missionaries and some Chinese scholars feel that the trinity was mentioned, that Yahweh is inferred, and that a "great sage would come who would bring knowledge and peace to all men." Is it possible that the world's religions are actually similar and not as different as supposed?

Certainly, when translating the *Tao Te Ching*, I was amazed that the writing and meaning had not only a deeply religious and spiritual text that we are accustomed to in western society, but were very similar to the Bible in many verses, and that other aspects of the *Tao Te Ching* and the Christian Bible are similar as well.

Next, it should be noted that the *Tao Te Ching* originated in two parts: the Tao Ching, which is in chapters 1–37, and the Te Ching, which covers chapters 38–81. When translating, I tried to stay as close to the original text as possible to make it understandable and bring new meaning, enlightenment, and freshness to those who read it.

Finally, I am hoping that this readable text I present will open discussion between people and help us all understand each other in a world that tends to criticize differences or that which we do not understand. So enjoy this book, apply its wisdom, and live in peace and love.

Chapter One

The great path that exists leads to heaven, but if you do not follow the great path, you are not following the eternal way. God is the beginning of heaven and Earth, and thus, the question is asked: What is your plan on Earth related to an unseen God? What is your plan to get to heaven? You must free yourself from your own desire to see God unwrap the mystery before you. He is the beginning, father, and mother of all things. You must free yourself from your own desires that bring problems. Without a solid plan to follow, evil consequences will result. In the beginning, you must make up your mind; will you follow good or evil? Then the question becomes, what is good and what is evil? Finally, what does God want for you? Put your trust in Him, for He reveals the secrets of all secrets and opens the gates for those who follow.

Chapter Two

To begin our journey, does it not make sense that we must live for God and not for our own desires? There can be no desire (wu-wei) as we flexibly take on what life presents to us without effort; it just is. God has a plan for us, and we should not judge a book by its cover, as all things are not as they appear to be. There will be good times and bad times, laughter and sorrow, and a blending of hardness and softness along the path to heaven. We cannot change it; we can only do our best in humbleness to follow the right path and to keep going.

Chapter Three

It's important to live humbly. There is no reason to brag about what you have and what others don't have. This only brings jealousy and sorrow, and others will want and crave what you have, but for what reason? These material things mean nothing, and bragging about what you have will result in people scheming against you to take your possessions. Also, never put people on a pedestal, as no one is better than anyone else. Instead, bring kindness and love to all, get them to relax, feed them, let them measure up, strengthen them, and you will not have to fear them.

Chapter Four

Following this spiritual path is exciting because it is full of knowledge, full of hope, and full of wisdom. The great path is the beginning of all things, and its resources are never-ending. It dulls the pain, dims the blinding light, and becomes one with the dust. Though it appears hidden, it brings love, gives love, and attracts love. It gives and receives compassion and togetherness, is overflowing in all of these things, and has been here forever. So stay on the great path.

Chapter Five

You are not just a speck of dust to God. You are not alone, nor does God take your walk with Him lightly. He knows your heart and your steps, and this path you will take, guided from heaven to Earth, is blended together along the journey you will live. Be sure that this is a path that is beyond just meditation, but one that must be experienced.

Chapter Six

Since God created Earth, there is also an important earthly component to help us understand ourselves and the terrain along the way. Some call it the "valley spirit," and others may refer to it as "mother earth," as these natural laws created from above flow without effort over time. Understanding these laws of nature is important when dealing with the root of Mother Nature and how it can benefit us or not, as it can be a friend or foe depending on the wisdom we have.

Chapter Seven

Earth is lasting, heaven is never-ending, and God reigns forever. They live in harmony to serve others, so they live forever. Likewise, those that put themselves last become first, and those who forget their own wants and serve others are protected because of their unselfish ways. By serving others, all your needs are met and are overflowing.

Chapter Eight

The greatness of the spiritual path is one that flows like water, which benefits life with very little resistance and is absorbed and experienced through all senses, even going to places where it is despised by some people. Goodness helps eliminate conflict. For example, a good house is built on the ground, and a good mind runs deep in thought. A good gift is kind. A good word is said with sincerity. A good ruler is fair. A good worker is ready to work. A good deed is well-received when it is well-timed. However, staying on the path and helping others do the same can be difficult, as men often hate what is good and love what is evil. So while on Earth, focus on what is good, move gently like a stream of water to help others by using gentleness and self-control and by setting an example to follow without coercion. If they still turn away, you will not be responsible for their fate. Always remember that goodness is grounded in kindness and sincerity.

Chapter Nine

Isn't it better to fill the pot of treasures much lower than the brim so it will not spill? Do you need that much extra? You may be sharp and on top today, but not tomorrow. So bragging about your riches, gold, jade, other material things, or your titles, and being puffed up with pride and boasting eventually means losing what you have. Focus on the right things in life. Putting in a good day's work to honor God is heaven's way.

Chapter Ten

Life is a give-and-take of strength and tenderness, of loving and letting go, of spiritual growth, and of putting away your desires to help the masses in an honest way. It is acting on spiritual knowledge, and yet guiding and raising others without force or ridicule or acting like a know-it-all. Do you understand this great virtue? Life is also about letting go of material things and focusing on the oneness of the path with the heart of a child who is happy just to be, while also living in balance with both love and the law as you consider others points of view fairly. Finally, always give without expecting something back, and do so with love.

Chapter Eleven

Life is short. Why fill your mind with things that do not matter? Keep an open mind, and be careful about what you put into it, as many things have a use. For example: Isn't the empty space in a bowl as valuable as the vessel itself? Isn't the open air coming through a window as valuable as the frame that shapes the window? So it is likewise with our thinking. Value comes from having a brain, but true value comes from not filling it with useless things. Instead, be open and receptive to what the path has to offer, which is of true value.

Chapter Twelve

In life, adding more ingredients does not create a better recipe, but it can spoil the taste and make it like garbage. More musical notes do not create better music, but they can create an annoying noise. More colors do not make a picture better, but they can smear the delicacy of the art. So remember that there has to be balance, and less is often more. Also, to eat too much, to hear too much, to see too much, and to gather too much takes you off the path. Be a king of living the life of self-discipline to reach heaven. Yes, heaven is the path to be sought, and the path is eternal for those who follow it, for in the end, even though the physical body dies, the spirit lives forever.

Chapter Thirteen

Avoid things that can take you off the path. Both praise and disgrace can cause fear because we can focus too much on the fear of success or the fear of failure, and it can take us off course. We fear when good things happen, we fear bad things may happen. So we must be disciplined, live without desire, and stay humble. We must be grounded in truth and therefore free from being ambushed with criticism, which often comes after you gain much acclaim or lose it all. We must also discipline our bodies for the long road ahead, and in doing so, we can care for the world. So continue on the right path, be at peace with yourself, and be a servant, for if you help the world with your service, the world shall respond in kind.

Chapter Fourteen

The great spiritual path cannot be seen, heard, or touched, and may seem elusive, but when looking for it, when listening for it, when reaching for it, those three things become one, and even though it is beyond physical grasp, it fills the soul. There is no light above it, and no darkness below it. It is beyond description. It is shapeless and colorless, and will exist from beginning to end of time. No matter where you start, you cannot see where it begins, and when you follow it, you cannot see where it ends. The path has not changed from the beginning, so master it, hold tightly to it in the present, and learn its history. This is both the spirit itself and the beginning of the path. Yes, this is the way.

Chapter Fifteen

Those who mastered the great path in the past did so wisely, and therefore, experienced the spirit and path in a profound way almost too difficult to believe. They mastered various traits to make the journey successful, like moving across a river in the winter. This is like the humbleness of a visiting guest carefully stepping as though the ice would give way, living simply with few possessions like uncarved wood, proceeding with caution, even in subtle obscurity, and being wary of those things that could take them off course. They were also kind, receptive, genuine, open to others, and continually took unclear teaching and made it clear and simple to all without the desire for personal gain. Learn from these wise past teachers as an example of the path you should follow.

Chapter Sixteen

There is value in just existing and being in touch with yourself. Empty your mind of foolish things, be still, and experience the great path, which will lead you to flourish and give you the eternal hope of heaven. Yes, when the spiritual path is embraced, you will be exalted and on your way to heaven. So do much with the little you have, and do much for others, for if you plant a seed in others, it will grow and be rewarded. There are times to be quiet in thought and reflection, and times to be sharing and more active on the journey. The path is impartial, so acting on one's own wishes instead of the path does harm. Be receptive to the great path, for it leads to the kingdom of heaven, which is the way, and the way is eternal.

Chapter Seventeen

To be a great leader requires the development of trust, but sometimes, you cannot tell by looking at a ruler's people what he is really made of. That is because some will love and praise him, some will fear him, and some will actually despise him. Therefore, the development of trust is a critical two-way street between a leader and his people. It is like the path itself, for in the olden days, this spiritual path had been known, loved, praised, and feared, while some hated it. It is not easy to follow, so trust in the wise leader and the path will be built over time. The great ruler must be sincere and careful with his words and work well with others so they feel that it was a team effort, not just the ruler taking the credit for reaching certain accomplished goals. That way, all can share happily in the reward. A leader must earn their trust, and by doing so, he can put people on the right path.

Chapter Eighteen

Be careful, for some will try to divert your way from the path with deception masked as intelligence, false benevolence masked as justice, or with false knowledge masked as wisdom. Yes, when there is an attempt to destroy the path by the foolish intellect of some who claim they know the way, there is a loss of compassion, and chaos and false teachers come forth. Good intention is no substitute for the great spiritual path that you have been given.

Chapter Nineteen

In life, people try to get by on their own limited knowledge, with their own duty as they see it, and with an eagerness to make a profit by trying to be clever. This is a shallow way to live. This breaks up families and attracts the wrong people. Instead, get rid of false piety and morality while claiming higher wisdom. Where there is false giving to impress, those who horde riches will succumb to robbery. To sum this up, see the path in its truest form so you will not be greedy with desire, and always remember to hang onto the purity of the path.

Chapter Twenty

So many people live with dread, while some are living in joy. But on the great path, you must keep going even when you feel weary and others appear to have plenty. You may sometimes feel like an outcast, alone without direction, but the right path must be experienced and applied, not just learned. Do not spend time dwelling on the unanswered questions of the world. Instead, focus on the journey itself, which requires sacrifice. Consider this: I am everywhere without a home, while others live happily with false joy. I may feel alone and tired, while other people enjoy treasures here, but I leave material possessions behind to follow the path. While these people seem happy and noticed, I am ignored. It seems that I have no place to rest, and everyone has their own goals. I may not understand this totally, and I know I am different, but I also know that I am carried by the root of the path for my benefit.

Chapter Twenty-One

The greatest virtue one can have is to follow the great path completely, even though it may seem hard to understand and vague. The great path has had form, substance, and real, life-giving essence for all who seek. From the beginning to the end, it does not get lost, and is always remembered. So keep this in mind: The good path can be followed, but cannot be described in true form and may seem obscure to some. It's indescribable with a vastness of knowledge driven by faith and belief. From the beginning of time to now, it has been around forever. Follow as closely to the center of the path as possible, for it gives you sustenance as the very essence of life, and it will be there for you like a trusted friend.

Chapter Twenty-Two

The path has all the answers for those who seek and are simplistic in their approach. One comes to recognize this and becomes an example for all. The path is already complete and perfect; it does not need to force its way, brag, or desire, and it is not contentious. Believe in its completeness and follow it. Therefore, simplify your life; get rid of the excess, which holds you back. Open your mind to the great path so you can be renewed. Be an example for all, which means not boasting, singing your own praises, or showing off to make a good impression. Then you will be held in high esteem.

Chapter Twenty-Three

Sometimes it is better to observe, be of few words, and go with the flow of the spiritual path. Also notice that even heaven and Earth often choose not to make it rain all day or make the winds persist. With this in mind, remember that you cannot change things by going off the path. Don't try to change the world and create continuity. Instead, focus on the path, and you and the path will become one and the same. Be careful: Just like someone would become married to the wrong path, and either path may appear to be a happy way to go, only one path is correct because people will only trust those on the right and true path. So remember, when you are one with the virtue of the great path, you will be welcomed and your deprivation will actually be turned into gain.

Chapter Twenty-Four

It is hard to balance yourself when standing up on your toes. Do not make yourself bigger than you really are with false bravado, bragging, and praising your greatness to others. Why? Because people see through this, and it does not last. You only destroy your inner-self and lose respect from others. Instead, stay balanced, don't stray from the path, keep a low profile, don't confront people, don't brag, and stay humble. It is useless to go another way; it only feeds the ego and is disliked by all. Those who follow the true spiritual path do not do this.

Chapter Twenty-Five

The spiritual path was born before heaven and Earth, and continues on as the "great path." This path is greatness that transcends time and place, continually flowing and never ceasing. Therefore, in the end, four things remain great: the spiritual path, heaven, Earth, and the supreme ruler who guides his people. This is because humans depend on the earth, the earth is dependent on heaven, and heaven is dependent on the spiritual path, which came from the beginning of God, who is the way.

Chapter Twenty-Six

Be still instead of impulsive. Bare your heavy burdens, knowing that when you reach your destination, like a man carrying his luggage, you will eventually find a place to rest and discover all that you need. So be prepared. For example, if a ruler had a thousand chariots and reacted with haste and took things lightly, what would he achieve? What could he lose? To act unwisely would be to lose mastery over yourself. Bare your heavy burdens, for the path is not easy. Don't be distracted by things of this world; instead, focus on what needs to be done. Otherwise, you lose the very foundation you and your family have, and the ability to lead or show others the path.

Chapter Twenty-Seven

Good travelers move around without leaving negativity. Their speech does not look for faults. Someone fair does not rely on a counting machine to pay fairly. You need not lock your door if your close relationships are friendly. The true, genuine binding to others needs no rope to hold it in place and will not come untied. God saves his people; he does not abandon anyone. Following him means to follow the light and to help others. One person who is enlightened teaches someone who is not, teaching him the way. Someone may think that they have knowledge, but if they do not follow and value the teacher, it shows that they are confused. This teaching is the essential essence of life. Again, treat people well and don't create stress with fault-finding, and people will accept you. In so doing, you can elevate them by lighting their path. Again, it is imperative that those on the right path must teach those who are not. You must first value and love these people to accomplish this.

Chapter Twenty-Eight

Do you know yourself? Do you know others? Learn from the masculinity within and around you, but cling to the woman. This is how it has always been. Approach life with the love and curiosity of a child. Be a model for others, living with humility and honor, and these virtues will take you to the finish line. If you get off track, return to the path. Live with the simplicity and the untouched beauty of uncarved wood, for carved wood will just be used as a tool by others. My friend, be strong, gentle, non-judgmental, and open with people. Be balanced, be an example, and stay on the path, and your path will be abundant. Finally, listen and be one with the path, and your path becomes whole.

Chapter Twenty-Nine

The world was created by God and is sacred, so how foolish is it for others to try to rule it? Those who try will fail, it will slip from their grasp, and they will be punished. God eliminates those who pursue arrogance and extravagance in an ever-changing world. Look around; some lead and some follow. Some are hot and some are cold. Some are strong and some are weak. Some succeed and some fail. How can you take over the world when the world spins indifferent directions? Don't look to rule the world, otherwise you will fail because of your greedy manipulating. Remember, sometimes things go right, sometimes things go wrong, and that's just the way it is. Therefore, stay away from excess, over-estimating your ability, and trying to be great, thus becoming overbearing. Instead, stay on the path.

Chapter Thirty

Using weapons and war against others in a prolonged fashion is the way to dig your own grave. Your troops will be bogged down in weeds and thorns, which will be followed by heartbreak and famine. Even a good commander knows when simple victory is enough and resolutions of peace can be reached. Solutions are best when they are absent of arrogance, pride, domination, and bragging. When pride enters and victory is overexalted, these strong things become old and complacent, and the end is near. This way is contrary to the spiritual path you must take. Using the great spiritual path always ensures a fair give-and-take. As I said earlier, if you go to war with people, you dig your own grave. Learn quickly and stop this action. Yes, it is good to achieve, but don't brag about it. Achieve in humbleness without forcing your way with others, because when you do brag, you are on the wrong path.

Chapter Thirty-One

Using weapons is an unfavorable thing to do. No one likes them, and the man on the wise path does not use them if at all possible. In peacetime, honor the left side. When going to war, honor the right. Make your position one of peace and not war if you can, as this is the better position. However, if you must go to war, the second-in-command stands to the left, and the commander-in-chief stands to the right to carry out plans properly. There should be no delight in killing because you cannot achieve your true goals this way. Only those who like to kill are happy to use weapons, but no one will trust them. This is because regular citizens have to bury their own and will have to shed tears, which leads to further distrusting those above them who use weapons.

Chapter Thirty-Two

The great spiritual path needs no title, yet moves forward in its greatness. What a world we would have if the greatest of rulers and the entire world could follow it. What reign of joy that would be! Heaven and Earth would unite, and all would live in complete harmony without being asked. However, they could not, so rules were made and names given to all. Those who stay within the guidelines of the path avoid danger, so follow the great spiritual path, which is similar to the stream that flows to the river, which flows to the ocean. Also, don't worry about having a title for yourself, because if the great path itself does not need a big name or title to follow it, neither do you. Live bravely, have no fear, but don't be misled. Remember that many things will fall into place, and then eventually, heaven and Earth will have balance and the heavens will open up. Some will be unable to cope and make adjustments to follow the path, causing divisions among you. Knowing to stay on the path will help you avoid falling into these situations.

Chapter Thirty-Three

If you understand others, you are intelligent. If you understand yourself, you are wise. To overcome others is power. To overcome yourself is to be among the mighty. To not be envious of people, and be content with what you have is to be rich. Those who don't stray from the path show persistence and resolve. If you live with energy and passion, and hold nothing back in following the path, you live forever. Though you may die an earthly death, your life will go on.

Chapter Thirty-Four

The great spiritual path cannot be stopped; it is like a large flood reaching both left and right. All things depend on its existence. It helps to clothe, feed, and help others without seeking reward or wanting to rule over them. The great path is without desire, and those who return to it are rewarded. Without striving to be called great, great things can be accomplished. Therefore, the great spiritual path cannot be stopped. At times, it requires much to survive, but again, it cannot be stopped, only slowed temporarily. So if you get sidetracked, return to it, and it will show why it is great.

Chapter Thirty-Five

Hold to the great spiritual path, and the world will follow you without wanting to do harm. In fact, it will bring rest and a joyful peace. However, be wise; those who just speak about the path but do not follow it miss the splendid spice of the path. Their words are empty and tasteless. Don't be distracted, for those who follow wine, food, and pleasure are distracted, which brings emptiness. The right path is what you feel, the spirit, the way, and it's there for the taking. The great path cannot be seen or heard, but its force is never exhausted.

Chapter Thirty-Six

Take stock of who you are; those things that need to be shrunken in your life should first be expanded and examined so they do not come back. Your weaknesses must be addressed so they become strengths. Cherish your last vices, then get rid of them. Help others by discarding what you do not need. Develop your soft and tender side, which overcomes those who are hardened and strong. Develop clarity inside of yourself. Say goodbye to the old and hello to the new. Like fish in deep waters, you cannot reach everyone. Keep all weapons in their sheaths whenever possible, and live in peace. Choose your battles carefully, and move forward on the path.

Chapter Thirty-Seven

The great path is not in doing, but in being, and it encompasses and accomplishes all. If leaders embrace it and abide by it, it will transform them. When their own unnatural wishes appear, they must be subdued with the simplicity of the path so they can be freed from their own desires and filled with the stillness and peace of the right spiritual way. This is how the world will settle this issue. So remember, leaders should embrace the great path and keep an open mind rather than trying to force themselves unnaturally in the world. If they can do this, and they follow the right path, heaven will be pleased.

Chapter Thirty-Eight

Those with high moral standards are self-evident to all. Those with low moral standards really have no standards at all. Those with high virtuous standards do not need to pretend, but simply are themselves. Those with low virtuous standards have to pretend to be someone else, may have false motives, and have to work on themselves. Those with true benevolence act kindly, try to do good things, and give generously without repayment. Those who just act righteous usually come with an agenda, and if they don't get what they want in return, they often try to manipulate and use force against others. This is why the path is so important. When people get off the great path, they just depend on virtuous acts. When that doesn't work, they depend on some benevolence. When that doesn't work, they work on appearing righteous. When that doesn't work, they become symbolic through rituals, which is where all honesty ends and utter confusion begins. Those with superficial knowledge of the way just have flowers in their hand from a tree that bears fruit. Clinging to the flowers alone represents future problems. Those who abide by the greatness of the path become fruitful. They keep the fruit and reject the flower. Therefore, being moral on the surface is not real morality. Pretending to be nice and putting on airs is false. True goodness and morality is not manipulative or done for selfish reasons. If you pretend to have a person's best interests at heart and don't, they will become angry with you. If you appear to be loyal and sincere and aren't, it will anger people. The deepness and thoroughness of being real and getting to know the whole situation instead of what a situation appears to look like is important.

Chapter Thirty-Nine

Oneness in life is important. Heaven is united, and things become clear. Unity on Earth is created, and it becomes solid ground. The great spirit unites to create a deity. The valleys unite to create abundance. All things unite to create life. Great rulers unite and look after the world. They all have unity because of God. If this did not happen, the sky would tear apart, the earth would crumble, the deity would wither, the valleys would dry up, life would perish, and rulers would be defeated. Therefore, be humble and be better than no one else. Be one with them. This is why some great rulers sometimes feel alone and unworthy, but make the most of humility. Throw off the pretense and sparkle of jade, and seek to be like a regular rock. Let me sum up. Wholeness is oneness. God's path is clear. While life on Earth is rough, the peace and spirit of the path will fill the voids and lead to wholeness in life when it is led by compassion and effective rulers, as God does not want division. Without the path, Earth would not be strong and peaceful, things would vanish, and rulers would be ineffective. If you think of yourself as humble and follow the path, greatness can develop because of the lack of desire for material things and pretense.

Chapter Forty

Coming home and back to the great path is done through the movement of the spirit. Yielding back to the path is also part of the cyclical nature. Like in nature, many things are birthed from a being, yet in the beginning, a being came from the birth of a non-being or spirit. So come home, back to the path, because it softens the burden of the road ahead. It takes you on a journey from birth to personal existence and from a non-being to a being, keeping you on the great path of wisdom.

Chapter Forty-One

The path is so rewarding because it is not easy to follow. To those on the outside, at times, it may seem dimly lit, sometimes retreating, like a curved path, low on virtue, and where the highest virtue seems lacking. Even the pure whiteness seems stained, and some are seen as fragile and deficient and inconsistent. Even the great square has no corners, and the greatest vessel takes time to complete. Even the great image appears to have no form or shape to it, and the way seems to be hidden. Yet, look again; it is the great path that gives and nourishes and completes your journey! Think of it like this: Superior students hear the path and follow it. Some in the middle hear it and sometimes follow it, but sometimes fail to do so. A third group that doesn't understand it just laughs it off, and if they didn't laugh, it would not be the great path! Perhaps this is because the path is not easy, but long and tedious, and requires sacrifice and sometimes standing alone to be able to reach the true self in a changing world that we explore to the ends of the earth. It takes a long time to master the path, and sometimes, this good news that the path represents is hard to grasp and mysterious to some. So always follow the right path.

Chapter Forty-Two

In the beginning, the great path produces one. Then one gives birth to two, then two give birth to three, and then these three are the beginning to giving birth to all things. Then it continues on forward, carried by yin and embracing yang to achieve harmony by blending together their energy and vital breath. However, the path is not easy, but they fight on, fearful of being alone, desolate, and unworthy. The rulers have the same fears, and these people come to realize that in life, you can benefit from loss and lose from gaining. I will teach what others before me taught; those who use force and violence will not die from natural causes. This will be the foremost doctrine of what I teach. So remember that yin and yang will yield to each other to keep harmony in a divine or God-like way. Some may lose what they don't need or is not good for them. Some may gain something, whether it be a material possession or a desire that may hurt them. Impulsive force, demanding its own way, leads to demise.

Chapter Forty-Three

Look around. The softest and gentlest things of the world overcome the hardest and most stubborn. Sometimes no words are needed, and yet the spirit can penetrate and get inside that which seems to have no openings. Ah! So I now know the value of taking no action, the value of teaching with no words, and yet still accomplishing much, and yet this is understood by so few in the world. So remember that gentleness overcomes strife. The spirit moves, and you must react to the world in a positive way without personal gain to help others; this is important. In the end, some of the best teaching we can do is without words, but by being a model for those who want to follow and observe our gentleness.

Chapter Forty-Four

What is important to you: being famous and accumulating things, or being who you actually are and can be? What is more important: accumulating great wealth, or being comfortable with who you are and what you have? What is really worth more, and what is worth less? Is it gain or loss? You can gain great fortunes that are accumulated through greed, but it will soon be lost, so be satisfied with what you have because there is no disgrace in being content. Gather just what is required to fill your needs and you avoid being harmed and will endure much longer. Always remember that the useless or unnatural desire of material possessions and accumulation of things can come back to haunt you. Having balance and knowing when to say "enough is enough" is an important lesson to learn.

Chapter Forty-Five

Even those who seem the most perfect have flaws, and those who seem to have everything are lacking. They always seem to have plenty and never run out, but their abundance seems empty. The fact is that nobody is perfect. Those who appear the most straight are bent, and those with the greatest of skills can appear awkward. The most eloquent of speakers stumbles over his words now and then. However, you can overcome. By moving, you overcome the cold. By keeping still, you overcome the heat. By looking inside, you will find that peace and quiet rule the world. So always remember that trying to be perfect without seeing the bigger picture of clarity and peace is useless. The path may not seem grand to some and contradictory to others, and it requires walking a narrow path, but seeing the path and becoming one with it is everything.

Chapter Forty-Six

When the world follows the great path, fields are fertile, the harvest is abundant, and great horses till the soil. When the world fails to follow the path, these warhorses are used on the field of battle. Sadly, there is no crime greater than to be filled with greedy desires. There is no bigger disaster than to be discontented. So here is the great lesson: find contentment, which leads to great satisfaction. Remember, when the path is followed, there is peace, and the country is not preparing for war. Realize that current suffering is enough, be content with what you have, and remember that greed takes you off the great path.

Chapter Forty-Seven

Look inside and you will know the world without stepping out your door. Without looking out the window, you know the great spiritual path to heaven. Isn't it ironic that the farther one travels, the less one knows? Therefore, the wisest of the wise knows without traveling, perceives without having to look, and achieves without acting. No special education is needed to know the path and the way to heaven. In fact, the more experience you have sometimes shows that less is known. Wise people learn this quickly.

Chapter Forty-Eight

Those who seek knowledge add something important to their lives every day. Those who pursue the great path let go of more and more things they don't need, until no more action is needed. With nothing more to do, nothing is left undone. Remember, the goal is not to continually interfere or tamper with the world because those that try are not fit to take over the world. When knowledge is gained by following the path, you let go of the things you no longer need while gaining new wisdom. These old things are left behind. Part of this self-actualization, of being all you can be, is peace. So let the world be, and don't manipulate it for personal gain. For if you act on your desires to conquer the world, you could lose your soul."

Chapter Forty-Nine

The wise ruler makes decisions by keeping the concerns of his people in mind. He treats those who are both good and not good the same, with the virtue of goodness in his heart guiding him. He treats those who are both faithful and unfaithful the same, with the virtue of faithfulness to them in his heart. The wise ruler lives in harmony with the world as much as possible, and so the people turn their attention to him with open ears and open eyes, because he treats them like his own children. Remember, many are trying to do their best, so have no grudges, but compassion and forgiveness for people. Don't expect too much and you won't be disappointed. God loves you unconditionally, so follow this same path.

Chapter Fifty

In life, we travel from birth to death. People also choose different paths. For example, three out of ten choose a normal life, three out of ten choose death and its sorrow, and still another three out of ten race through life, experiencing excess and expecting too much from life. However, I have heard that there is one who truly knows how to live. During his travels, he does not encounter the rhinoceros or the tiger. He can pass through an enemy battlefield and not be struck by weapons. In him, the rhino has no place to thrust his horn. The tiger has no place for its claws. The soldiers have no place to use their blades. Why? This is because death itself has no place in him. Remember, many spend their life of activity in taking the wrong road or reaching for the pleasures of life that do not fulfill it. Therefore, live life with great passion, cautious intelligence, and courage, and you will find your way, protected by the great path.

Chapter Fifty-One

The great path gives birth to its followers. Their nourishment is virtue. They are shaped by matter. The conditions around them are perfect and make them whole. Therefore, there is no one that doesn't revere the great path and value its virtue. It is not because they demand their way, but because of who they are and the nature of their being. This path gives them birth, nourishes them, raises them, nurtures them, protects them, matures them, and takes care of them. It produces life without failing them. It helps them without flaunting over them. It nurtures them without dominating them, for this is the spiritual virtue of the great path. Yes, the inspirational path is the beginning that raises, guides, punishes, protects, and gives meaning and quality to life in a way that is valuable and without coercion or force. All of this is the spiritual virtue of the great path.

Chapter Fifty-Two

We can compare the beginning of the path to the children that spring forth and follow their mother. If we know that the mother is on the right path, then we know that the children are as well. We also know that if they cling to their mother who comes forth from the very beginning, the children will not be harmed their entire lives. Keep things sealed, including your lips, and there will be little turmoil, and you will be free from exhaustion. Look at the small details for clarity. Find the softness in others, which is a strength. Shine a light on things until they become clearer, and then you will have no misery by living this way eternally. It can be said that the path begins, and out springs the fruit of this growth, so stay close to the path until you die. Don't get involved and meddle in mundane things; instead, keep your focus and light on the path and take time to notice the small things, but be flexible so you will be both gentle and wary of the road ahead.

Chapter Fifty-Three

If I have just a little common sense, I will follow the great path. My only fear is that I stray from it. Although the great path goes straight ahead, many people prefer to deviate from it and take their own path. For example, the palaces of great rulers shine mightily, but the fields are barren with weeds and the warehouses are empty. These so-called leaders wear expensive garments, carry sharp swords, feast on food and drink, have more wealth than they need, rob others, and are filled with vanity, but let me say this: this is not the way to go, and this is not the great path! Always remember that the great path involves sacrifice, so be wise about your choices, and don't take shortcuts. Some spend time with wine, women, and song, and only care about themselves and their riches. This is not the path to take.

Chapter Fifty-Four

The great path is something that is well-planted and cannot be uprooted. A strong hold prevents escape. Children and all their descendants that follow will never stop praising it. True virtue is cultivating the path in yourself, so cultivate it in your family, and it becomes overflowing in abundance. Cultivate it in the city, and the virtue lasts. Cultivate it in the country, and the virtue prospers. Cultivate virtue in the world, and look, the great path is universal! Always take the great path because it has been around for a long time, it will guide you, and it won't slip from your grip if you follow it. In fact, the worshipping of this path has been carried on from previous generations, so take this path and spirit and pass it to your family, to your city, to the country, and to the world.

Chapter Fifty-Five

Those who have an abundance of great virtue are similar to the youthfulness of a blessed newborn infant. Bees, wasps, and scorpions do not sting him. The snake does not bite him. Birds of prey and wild beasts do not attack him. Though his bones are soft and his muscles are weak, look at his grip; it is firm! By reflex and without knowledge of a union between man and women, his loin rises to maximum height. He can shout or cry all day, and never grow hoarse. He optimizes his harmony, which remains constant. This consistency leads to more eternal clarity. His vitality is visibly present. Power is achieved by using his mind to control his vital breath. Yet those without virtue are put on a pedestal and soon decay. They appear strong but grow old. Those who love contrary to the great path and go against the wise road soon perish. Remember, those that have morals, use fairness, and have character are without attack.

The grip of the path gives lasting power and gives rise to harmony. It illuminates and nourishes life because of self-control. It helps people to grow, for otherwise, they die. The great path is blossoming, growing, and leads to life. The non-path leads to death. Choose wisely.

Chapter Fifty-Six

Those who know, do not speak. Those who speak, do not know. So seal the lips. Shut the doors. Dull all sharp things. Untie all knots. Dim the spotlight. Become one with dust, which is a spiritual union. Those who obtain this special knowledge will not be seduced or abandoned and will not be unduly favored or neglected. They will also not be unduly honored or humiliated. Therefore, the world bestows honor and esteem on them. Each person will be responsible for every idle word they speak, so speak without anger; instead, speak for peace or be silent. In this way, you benefit from non-action, for even if you are right, you can cause strife even though others that speak do not know what they are saying. It's not worth it to prove them wrong. Let oneness be your goal, and the world will notice and respond.

Chapter Fifty-Seven

A country should be ruled by justice and integrity. A military does well when it has the strategy of surprise. Governing is best when less interference and less action is needed. How do I know this is true? When there are many restrictions in the world, the people become poorer. When sharper weapons are plentiful, more chaos will be there. The more cunning people are, the more clever tricks and strange occurrences that will arise. The more that laws pop up, the more robbers and thieves will show up. Therefore, the great leader says, I do not act, and the people reform themselves. When I stay peaceful, the people use fairness to lift themselves. When I do not interfere, the people become rich within themselves. I have no desire, and the people have the beauty of uncarved wood. Fairness wins the trust of the people, as does respecting those who oppose you. Accept the world without worry, and don't over regulate it. Too many laws, too many guns, more reliance on cleverness and deception, and the poor interpreting of laws can lead to anger and rebellion. If you can live in peace, serenity, and without forcing your way, the people around you will make good choices.

Chapter Fifty-Eight

When the government does not interfere, the people are simple and pure. When the government pries into their lives, the people become shrewd and learn to connive. It is this misery that rests upon their happiness, and this happiness that peaks out from this misery. Where does it end? What is the outcome where correctness becomes a liability, where goodness is a burden, and the people become long-suffering with confusion? Therefore, rulers should govern with sharpness, but without cutting. They should point things out, but not pierce. They are straightforward, but do not offend. They shine a light, but are not flamboyant. Rulers should relax and let people be. This constant criticizing, micromanaging, fault-finding, and even greed can ruin the good will among the people. The wise leader is able to get things done, correcting in a gentle way without fault-finding.

Chapter Fifty-Nine

Being conservative and doing things in moderation is key when ruling people and serving heaven. It helps to stop you from going the wrong way, and puts the focus on accumulating many virtues. When you gain many virtues, there is nothing you can't overcome. You will be unlimited in what you can accomplish. Then, with no limitations, you can rule the country. He who rules like a mother will last a long time. This means ruling with deep roots and a firm foundation. This is the great path for longevity and enduring clarity. Use good judgment and be careful with your resources, and you can overcome anything. This will bring confidence to people and allow you to be an effective, welcomed leader. This first begins with planting the roots of the path in the people.

Chapter Sixty

Ruling a great country is like cooking a small fish; you must not overdo it. Follow the great path to manage the world, and demons and ghosts will have no power, and the people will not be harmed. Therefore, if this evil cannot harm the people, and its ruler does not harm the people, there is a restoration and unity of virtue. Always remember, rule with the great path and wisdom in mind, and evil will be lessened and will not harm.

Chapter Sixty-One

The greatest country is like the smooth, lowest part of the river. It is like a gentle, receptive female and where the world begins. It is similar to a female who always overcomes the male with a yielding, peaceful serenity that he cannot resist. Therefore, if a great country simply yields to a small country, it will conquer the small country. Yet, if the small country yields to a great country, it will also be conquered by the great country. So depending on the greatness of the country, yielding can mean conquering or being conquered. However, both the large and small countries wish to serve the people, so for both countries to get what they need, the larger country should yield to the smaller one. This happens when they come together and are servants to each other, which produces gain. Always remember, people who want to work together will prosper, so think of others before yourself.

Chapter Sixty-Two

The great path provides all things. It is the source of treasure for the good person who is faithful, and even provides refuge for the struggling, unkind person. Remember, noble words can be exchanged and noble deeds and actions earn respect, therefore, why abandon the unkind person when there is hope? When the emperor is crowned and three high-ranking officials are installed, rather than offering jade carried by four horses, nothing can be compared to offering the great path as a gift. Why did the ancient people praise and revere the great path? Does it not say that those who seek will find, and that you can be saved from your wrongs? Therefore, the world recognizes and praises the great path for its tremendous value. Remember, the great path of wisdom is already known by its worth. You can find peace there, as deeds and words will help with the oneness of the path. Great kings and riches cannot help you like the wisdom found on the great path. The path is without human desire, so it has great worth.

Chapter Sixty-Three

Greatness comes from the ability to act without taking action. It is the ability to pursue together without interfering, and the ability to taste without tasting. How do you treat people? Try making small people seem big, and repay hatred and animosity with virtue and kindness. Plan ahead, and break down the difficult tasks so they become easy. Take care of the small problem before it becomes a bigger issue. Even the most difficult task begins with simple steps. The biggest thing in the world started small. Therefore, the great, wise man never strives for greatness, but always achieves it. Also, those who lightly make promises will never be trusted, and those who don't plan and consider things lightly will encounter great difficulty. Therefore, the wise man who plans ahead and sees everything as potential trouble often avoids difficulty. In summary, get sincerely involved without acting or pretending. Make an honest evaluation of the situation, and respond to evil with good. In doing so, you can correct the situation early, before the problem gets too big. Eliminating problems while they are small means success. Do not delay; treat everything as a project of difficulty that needs to be dealt with quickly.

Chapter Sixty-Four

Peace and serenity are easy to maintain, and with no disruption, it is easy to move forward. However, if the peace is brittle, it is easy to shatter. If peace is small and isolated, it is easy to scatter. Therefore, quickly act on anything that disrupts the peace before chaos arises. Success and growth come from a small but persistent place. For instance, the tree that is as wide as a man's embrace started as a mere sapling. A nine-story tower arises from a pile of dirt, and a journey of many miles begins with one step. The one who acts and interferes will fail, and the one who seizes will lose. Therefore, the wise man does not act unnecessarily or interfere, so he does not fail. He does not seize, and therefore, does not lose. So keep going and don't let up, for people often fail at the brink of success. Be as careful at the end of your business as you are at the beginning, and there will be no failure. Also, wise men live without desire for earthly treasure and goods. They acquire knowledge by not learning the wrong things. They help people redeem themselves and recover, and they assist nature but do not interfere. Think of it this way: Some things in life are obvious and well explained. So it is with handling projects. Act early before you dig a hole for yourself. Yes, start early, and do not wait until it is too late. Otherwise, you will have to rush to finish a project because of no or poor planning, and that usually ends in failure. So again, be as careful and as thorough in the beginning of doing something as you are at the end, and you will have success. Remember, the good leader not only plans, but puts desires aside, learns the hearts of people, and helps them without acting like their boss.

Chapter Sixty-Five

In ancient times, those who followed the great path did not share all their knowledge. Instead, they tried to use their cleverness to keep people uninformed, and thus stole from the people. This means that those who tried to rule by using knowledge in a clever way ruined their country with unfairness, while those that tried to rule fairly blessed their country with wisdom. Always know that there are two standards to consider, and knowledge of this is a profound virtue. In fact, this great virtue is far-reaching and is not about earthly treasures, but about bringing back all things to a great, congruent order. So speak with honesty and clarity. If you use deceit, you cheat the people, and these lies will catch up with you. People follow those with integrity, even though telling them what you think they want to hear sounds better.

Chapter Sixty-Six

The great river and ocean can be the kings of a hundred valleys because they lie below them. Therefore, think of it this way: If a great ruler wants to stand above and speak for the people, he must first lower himself before them and be humble. If a ruler wants to lead people, he must get behind them and follow them. Then, even though the ruler stands above the people, they feel no oppression, and when he leads people, they feel no barrier. The world naturally lifts and exalts this type of leader and never grows tired of him. Why? Because he does not confront or resist the people, therefore, no one in the world resists him. Consider the volume of the seas; this equates to the volume of support from people if a ruler speaks with humbleness and doesn't oppress them, for not only will they accept him, they will clamor for his leadership. Be this kind of ruler.

Chapter Sixty-Seven

The entire world says that the great path is greater than anything else. Nothing can compare to it. Even if something could be compared to it, it still would have been insignificant a long time ago. There are three things that I cherish and count as treasures. The first is compassion, the second is moderation, and the third is not being concerned about being the most important person in the world. With compassion, one has the ability to be brave. With moderation, one can still be generous. And by not claiming to be the most important person, one can still rule. However, being brave with no compassion, generosity, or moderation, or trying to rule by being the most important person around ends in death. Those who share compassion, even in battle, will be victorious. Those who defend themselves will remain safe. Heaven will save and protect those with compassion. To sum up, the path is great wisdom, so listen to it.

Remember to live with compassion and love, live within your means, live with no desire, and live with consideration for others. Don't think of yourself as better than others. Have empathy for others, and have something to give. Learn at your own pace, and do not rush ahead and claim superiority or brilliance. Life is not worth living without giving love and compassion to others. Rely on heaven to accomplish these things, and your compassion will be rewarded with compassion.

Chapter Sixty-Eight

The greatest of warriors are not violent. The best soldiers do not get angry. The greatest conquerors do not engage their enemies. The best leaders lower themselves before the people to serve them. This is called the great virtue of no confrontation. This is called the power of managing people to their proper tolerance and capacity. This is called the harmonious union with heaven. It is the perfected principles of the ancient people. To sum up, when approaching battle, be balanced, take no foolish risks, and keep your composure and wits about you. The best defense is one where attack or war is not needed. Treat these people as better than yourself and with respect as a counterattack. There is reward in appealing to a person's talent, defusing anger, and catching them doing something right. If you can do this, the heavens will rejoice.

Chapter Sixty-Nine

In the military, the great warrior says, "I dare not be the host, but prefer to be the guest on their land. I prefer to retreat a foot than dare advance an inch." This is called marching without marching. This is showing arms without using arms. It is the ability to charge with no enemy in front of me, and the ability to seize without using weapons. There will be no greater misfortune than to underestimate the enemy, for when I underestimate my opponent, I risk losing my treasure. When armies are evenly matched, the compassionate one will be victorious. Think of it this way: You must know when to move forward and when to retreat. You must know when to give ground in a debate or conflict. Keep your weapons hidden, because this surprise attack is where you can accomplish much without a fight. Finally, keep a proper respect for opponents, and don't take anyone for granted, for if you do, it could mean defeat.

Chapter Seventy

Though my words are easy to understand and easy to practice, the world cannot understand them or practice them. My words have a special origin. My deeds are principled and from above. Yet, because people do not understand this, they cannot understand me. Those few who understand me are why I am highly valued. It is like the wise man who wears plain clothes, but on the inside, he conceals jade. Consider this: These laws of wisdom come from experience and the way of the great path, yet many do not understand the path or practice its teachings. In fact, if all people were able to understand me, I would not be needed. But I am of great value to those who do understand me and don't follow their own desires. To the wise, my dress is simple, but on the inside, I am worth the value of great jade.

Chapter Seventy-One

The best path is understanding that you do not know everything, and by contrast, the wrong path is not knowing but thinking you do, which is self-induced illness. Truly, only when one sees his flaw as an illness can one get better. The wise men are not ill because they see their flaws as illness and try to be better. That is why they do not have illnesses. So don't be a know-it-all, admit your wrongs, and admit that you don't know everything, and you will earn respect. Not knowing and thinking you do is both arrogance and illness.

Chapter Seventy-Two

When people no longer fear the authorities, the overall greater dread and doom declines. Why? The wise leader does not limit his people or crowd their space. The wise leader does not reject their work or make his people weary. Because the wise ruler does not reject his people, they do not reject him. Therefore, the wise ruler knows himself, and avoids bringing glory to himself. He respects and cares about his being, but he does not heap praise upon himself. He is smart enough to discard one, and wise enough to choose the other. Therefore, lead without manipulation, and you will win the people to your side. Don't get into their personal business and use it against them to keep them down. If you understand this, it will help you respect yourself and those around you. The simple key is to let go of the desire to control the people.

Chapter Seventy-Three

Those that use their boldness to be daring shall die. Those that use their boldness wisely, but do not dare, survive. Of these two, one is a clear benefit and one is harmful. Who knows why heaven detests this daring? Even the wise man finds this difficult to understand, for the great path of heaven does not contend, but always wins. It does not speak, but certainly responds. It is not summoned, but knows when to come on its own. It may seem to be at rest, but it has an excellent plan. Heaven can cast a vast net, and while the netting may appear to be loosely meshed, nothing slips through. To sum up, if you have the choice between being brave and foolish together, or just being brave, pick being brave without taking silly risks. Why? Who knows? Even leaders can't understand heaven and its ways, but there is benefit to those who give freely without having to take foolish chances. So relax, be free of worry, and set goals. Reach out and listen to others. Heaven has a vast array of resources, but there is a right way to do it. Always combine your courage with intelligence.

Chapter Seventy-Four

If you come across people who aren't afraid of dying, why threaten them with death? If people live in constant fear of death and are punished by death for breaking the law, then who would dare? Remember, this is not your job, for there is already a supreme executioner in place. Trying to substitute for the master executioner is like trying to find a replacement for the master carpenter to carve wood. Very few could do so without injuring their hands. Therefore, don't make idle threats and constantly instill fear, for if you do, the people will come to hate you and revolt. Leave judgment and execution to a higher power, for this is not your job and is best left to someone else, otherwise you just harm yourself.

Chapter Seventy-Five

People are hungry because rulers take too much money with the taxes they force them to pay. That is the reason they starve. People are difficult to govern because of too much interference from their rulers. Seeing this, people take life lightly and revolt. They expect more from life, so they have no regard for death. In the end, those who live without worrying whether they will die are superior to those who tightly cling to the value of their own life. So remember this: People starve because of greedy rulers who demand high taxes, and if you create contempt in others, they will not fear you. Therefore, think of others, not just yourself, and be at peace.

Chapter Seventy-Six

People are born into the world being soft and flexible. When they die, the body becomes hard and rigid. Look at the grass and trees and all living things; they are soft, supple, and thriving while alive. When they die, however, they wither, becoming dry and brittle. It could well be said that those that follow the hard and stiff way are friends of death, but those that are soft and flexible are the companions of life. By that measure, the inflexible army cannot win, and the rigid tree will be chopped down. It could also be said that the big and rigid lie below, and the soft and flexible belong above. Remember to live your life as a child would, by being accepting, soft, open, and gentle, instead of being harsh, cold, bitter, and critical. As much as possible, be flexible in your position, instead of unwavering and cynical. There are two paths you can take: the path on Earth that leads to heaven, or the wrong path that can lead to hell.

Chapter Seventy-Seven

The great path of heaven is like stretching the bow back and adjusting. When the bow is too high, it is lowered, and when the bow is too low, it is raised to get back on target. Those things in excess are reduced, and things that are lacking are replenished. The great path of heaven in itself reduces the excess and replenishes the deficiency. Contrast that with the path the people take. They reduce even further the deficiency they have, and supply those that have an excess already. Yet, who has excess and supplies it to the world? Only the one who follows the great path. Therefore, the wise man acts humbly and does not take credit. He achieves without dwelling on it and bragging, and he does not display his worth. Think of it another way: Those who are able to give should do so, rather than the way of some, who become more and more greedy and either steal from the poor or don't help at all. So give generously with selflessness and without bragging.

Chapter Seventy-Eight

Behold, nothing in the world is softer or weaker than water. Yet nothing is more persistent in attacking and beating the hard and strong. Nothing can surpass water in its effectiveness or take its place. The weak can overcome the strong, and the soft overcomes the hard. Though everyone in the world knows this, few in the world can put it into practice. Therefore, the wise man says, the one who accepts the disgrace of the country can rule it and its resources. The one who accepts the problems and misfortunes of the country is set to be king of the world. Sometimes, true words seem to be false, so take a clue from the water, which is persistent with success, unlike the rock, which can be worn down by the flow of water. In the end, be persistent and gentle. Reject corruption, otherwise it will become your master. If you accept these facts, focus on the goal, and become like water, you will be a success.

Chapter Seventy-Nine

Even after hated rivals make peace, some resentment and bitterness remains. So how can this be resolved? It happens when the wise man honors his contract and word, but doesn't demand the other person fulfill his responsibility. It is important for those with virtue and honor carry out what is due, while those without virtue and honor sadly pursue money or others terms of their claim to the end. Fortunately, the great path has no favorites; it simply gives to those who are kind and compassionate. So let me remind you to not get angry and interfere into other people's business because these people will hold grudges and will not forget. In the end, keeping your promise means integrity, while broken promises mean a lack of integrity.

Chapter Eighty

The country is small with few people, and while they have many weapons, they do not use them, for they take death seriously and choose to live nearby rather than move far away. Though they have war boats and fighting carriages, they do not use them. Yes, there is plenty of weapons and armor, but there is no need to show it. Instead, they spend time tying knots on ropes. Then they savor their tasty food, they will be comfortable in their clothes, there will be peace in their homes, and their daily lives will be joyful. Sadly, even though they can see their neighbors and hear their roosters and dogs, they will grow old and die before even visiting one another. So don't forget what is really important. Value life and enjoy it. Protect yourself, and stay out of quarrels. Don't forget the simple way of life, for this is precious. Those who truly give people what they desire in terms of food, clothes, and shelter, will be at peace with their neighbor.

Chapter Eighty-One

True words are not always welcomed. Words that sound pleasing are not always true. Those who are doing right need not argue with others, and those who argue are not always right. Those who know the great path may not be highly educated, and often, many who are highly educated do not know the way. The wise man does not hoard things, for the more he has, the more he helps others, and the more he gives, the more he gains. To sum up, be simple in speech, and don't argue. Be focused on the simplicity of the path instead of the complexity of examination. Learn the path by experiencing it. Even these educated men are mere fools in their understanding, while those who are uneducated but still follow the path are the ones who understand all. Remember that we have a giving God, not a selfish God, who puts us on the right path, for heaven is here to help and not harm us. Follow the path of wisdom set forth here. Finally, always keep this in mind: The great path to heaven is for our benefit and does not harm us, but helps us. It does not contend against the wise man, but assists him. Always follow the great path.

About the Author

Kevin M. Thomas is an award-winning author with titles like *Tao Te Ching De-Coded* and *Why Daughters Need Their Dads*, and has a varied background in medicine, alternative health, counseling, religion, and mind-body healing. Kevin is passionate about promoting and delivering positive change to any person, and he strives to affect personal growth in individuals via mind-body-spirit research and application. Finally, he considers his relationship with God and his unconditional love for his children, Isiah, Caroline, Kimberly, and Cheyenne, as his greatest treasures.

Chinese Spiritual Thoughts

Chinese Spiritual Thoughts is more of a direct English translation of the *Tao Te Ching*, the second-most translated book in the world, and a basis for Chinese Religion and Philosophy. This book differs from author Kevin Thomas's previous versions of the *Tao Te Ching*, because where *Wisdom and Virtue* and the *Tao Te Ching De-Coded* were more paraphrased versions, and *The Great Path* was more of a modern interpretation of Lao Tzu's great classic, this book is a solid and direct English translation of one of the most important books in history—a book that can guide and inspire people on the great journey of life.

KETNA PUBLISHING: Kevin Thomas and Erik Naugle make up KETNA Publishing, a small, hometown publisher located in mid-Michigan. Their goal is to deliver high-quality information into the hands of the people so they can positively change their lives via body, mind, and spirit application. You can contact KETNA Publishing at kt123trailblazer@gmail.com or grobthom@aol.com or write to KETNA Publishing, P.O. Box 90861, Burton, Michigan, 48509.

www.ingramcontent.com/pod-product-compliance
Lightning Source LLC
Chambersburg PA
CBHW070631300426
44113CB00010B/1742